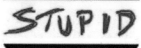

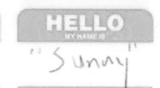

Dedicated to the weirdos...

And, dedicated to you.

INTRODUCTION

"Afoot and lighthearted I take to the open road, healthy, free, the world before me."

Walt Whitman

Hello! My name is...

Well.

Depends.

If you knew me as a kid, I was 'bright'.

before college, I was 'Toso'.

during, I'm probably 'Sanni'.

And if you happen to know me now; well.

I'm just crazy.

It's funny – how labels can follow you

Influence you for the better,

or trap you in a box of unwanted expectations.

Keeping you there for as long as you are willing to believe the lie.

I'm a naturally reclusive dude.

Could have easily hid away from the world and ceased all communication, but that would be too easy.

And, that's not what I want. I want what's difficult.

Meaning I want to know you.

And not just the good. But the bad too.

Then, I want to love you anyway.

I want folks to prove me wrong about what appears to be a depravity that plagues our human condition, I want them to show me that God is real by the way we treat each other. I want strangers to show kindness, and lovers to show love.

Basically, I want a restoration of collective decency, and an elevation of the norm to reflect the truths we hold self-evident.

I want a lot of things, I guess.

But now I realize –

What I have *really* wanted this whole time, was myself. My *real self.*

Buried under years of false expectations and half-baked relations...

to finally show his face.

And I think he's breaking free.

So, I'm here to give an account of my life to date.

A time stamp of sorts, to help me remember who I was, while remaining true to who I'm becoming.

You don't have to proceed.

But if you do – I hope you can get something from it.

And if not, well – sorry.

I am currently sitting in an unfamiliar room,

with a relatively uninspiring story.

So, the goal is not to entertain you.

The goal is to heal.

This is for me.

I landed in Brighton, England October 4th, 2019.

Moved out on a whim and without a plan.

Will be fresh out of cash in about a month. So, there's a valid argument to be had that I should be doing something else with my time other than finishing a book that won't sell.

But I'm not. Because I believe in miracles.

If you're reading this, it means at some level, you do too.

Perhaps you maintain that I'm a sane human being, or our friendship compelled you check it out, or maybe you don't like me at all.

Simply curious.

Whatever the reason, you're here.

And I don't believe in coincidences.

Which means, you right now, are reading these words – for a reason.

So, fair warning.

Unless you put this book down *now* – I will ensue to share with you my unadulterated truths – and it will be because our universe willed it to occur. Take from that what you may.

Because, money is *temporary*.

And knowledge is *fleeting*.

But, *wisdom* – to me, is the essence of true power.

So, in order to better inform myself of how to move henceforth on this plane of reality, I've decided to clarify the narrative.

Map it.

Calibrate it.

Then, move forward.

Can't find your how, or your what if you don't first discover your "why".

So that's what I'm trying to do.

Find my why.

(Shout out Simon Sinek.)

Anyway, here it goes.

My story.

Warts and all.

Enjoy.

CHAPTER 1:
LET'S BEGIN.

For last year's words belong to last year's language. And next year's words await another voice.

And to make an end is to make a beginning.

T.S. Eliot

Any fool can know. The point is to understand.

Albert Einstein

Evander Holyfield was crowned heavyweight champion of the world the night before.

And across the pond – in St. Mary's hospital,

(which is where it just so happens, British royalty is also birthed.)

I came into this world and joined in on the ranks of humankind.

Though, there was no celebration for my victory. In fact, there wasn't much of anything.

Just me, and mom.

I was born on a Sunday.

November 7th, 1993. In London England, to a single mother.

I was raised in an apartment two blocks from Chelsea's football stadium yet grew up an Arsenal fan.

And, though I'm from the UK where proper football reigns supreme, my favorite 'football' team remains the Chicago Bears.

Go figure.

I think these facts alone are a good indicator of where this story may go; but before we get ahead of ourselves – let's bring it back.

Back to my grandmother. Grace Francis – the matriarch of our clan, and whose name, I have tattooed on my arm – persevered through the arduous existence of a housewife to a husband who suffered from rampant infidelity. Apparently this was the norm back then.

My biological aunt and uncle cut ties and moved over to the United States from Nigeria back in the mid-90s.

This presented an opening up of a chance for me to join in on the 'American dream.'

At least in the eyes of my folks.

See, due to a piece of legislation that had passed a few years prior; children became elevated in the Visa lottery system, which also tends to help those related to said kid get a bump in the immigration process.

What's funny – is that the law was meant to help Irish families.

Well. You know how my people do shah.

Okay... let's begin. For real.

I'll start this story with none other, than my mother.

A supremely devout Christian woman who tends to teeter toward self-righteousness.

A radically dedicated parent who was also a bit too radical in her son's religious affiliation.

A detail-oriented cleanliness enthusiast (clean freak), who has a knack for authoritarian tendencies yet, is quite comfortable in solitude apart from the raucous of society.

Our relationship is one that's very layered and complex and cannot be easily surmised in a book, let alone a chapter.

Still.

She is beautiful, and she is loving... but, she is also scary.

A multifaceted woman with a bevy of needs, desires, heartbreaks, successes, and everything in between.

I say all this just to clearly illustrate the type of environment in which young Toso began to try and make sense of the world.

I'll leave all judgements to the reader.

With no male presence to balance mom's energies or take up her time, I was often the target of both her ire and her angst.

I remember a back when I'd literally sprint through the house trying to get away from the dreaded wooden spoon, only to be inevitably discovered under the blankets and met with an even heavier dose of spankings for having made her chase.

In some ways, much of my childhood felt like a cruel game of hide and go seek. Though to be fair, I was a little shit.

Regardless, I feared my mother ways that can be odd to some.

I mean, I'd start getting sweaty and my heart would damn near jump from my chest if I heard my full name yelled above a certain octave; and yet, I loved this woman at the *very* same time because, well.

She was all I had.

It may be tough to understand how the source of one's pain can also be a foundation of comfort – and frankly, I'm not asking you to, because I'm not even sure I understand it.

But, it is what it is.

Daddy Issues

Alright.

Now back to the dead-beat.

My pops, who mind you I have seen twice during my 26 years on planet Earth, is a married man.

Unfortunately for my mom, he's married to another woman.

Mohammed Kudu Haruna; from whom my name still derives, is a man who looks, talks and I suppose acts like I do - but at the time of my birth, he didn't want much to do with me.

It is not his fault, nor was it my mothers.

'Fault' is a funny word anyway... as if we can somehow draw out and assign ultimate culpability from our ounce of a perspective.

To me, as human beings with inherently narrow viewpoints, finding fault is more a function of our need to feel like we understand, than of any real sense of liability.

What is true, is that both my parents had agendas and motivations that culminated in actions and reactions.

Which culminated to me.

As I understand it, my mom wanted a child, my dad wanted my mom – and that was that.

I'm still unsure of all the details surrounding my conception, like what their relationship status was, or if I was expected by both parties; but frankly, I'm not too worried anymore.

Again – it is what it is.

Four years later and we hit right around '97-98.

My mother gave the greenlight for aunt and uncle to take me in and raise me as their own, in hopes she could tag along later.

I'm sure she had good intentions.

Stability, freedom, opportunities, a chance to have a father figure.

These and more probably went into the decision, but to this day I can't help but wonder if I was simply given up.

It isn't a fun place to dwell.

So, I usually don't.

But from that moment began what I believe to be a strained relationship based in half assed phone calls and passive aggressive texts.

Back to the topic

It's tough to overstate how life altering this move was.

I wasn't changing cities or visiting a different part of the country, I was flying 7 hours across an ocean to a place I'd no concept of.

Wasn't aware of it then, but looking back...

I can now begin to see how that move set the stage for me to grow into the person I'm becoming today.

Still don't get it fully, but what I do know is that mom has been instrumental in forming me to be the man God is calling me toward.

And so, for that I've got to say...

Thanks mommy.

I love you.

CHAPTER 2: FAKE SHIT

She had blue skin, and so did he.

He kept it hid, and so did she.

They searched for blue their whole life through,

Then passed right by - and never knew.

Shel Silverstein

Considering that I had a last name incongruent to the rest of my immediate family, and spoke with a strange accent...

The transition to American life was about as rough as it could get for an unsure four-year-old plopped in the bubble of a south-Chicago suburb.

Especially, an African booty scratcher like myself.

(nah, I ain't forget)

Throw in September 11, 2001, and suddenly my last name became a more engrained part of my identity than I ever wanted it to be.

'Mohammed'.

Oh great.

In terms of my voice, it was squeaky, but distinctly British.

So, by kindergarten I'd been picked on enough to understand I needed to change it.

Thus, began my journey with masks.

Hello, my name is Blankface

Depending on who I was speaking with, I could be anything or anyone. It almost felt like a superpower.

I'm sure many can attest to this phenomenon; code-switching is what the psychologists call it.

A tool for the culturally fluent to move about freely within any given social circle.

In my case, it was a tool for survival.

Must have been around 1st grade when I became as proficient as the other kids in speaking with my "American" accent.

But, as my participation grew, the true self I longed to know was being neatly buried under piles of social norms.

Teachers saw that I was smart from early on. Principle even recommended that I skip a grade.

Despite, I was held back by my adoptive parents for fear of further social ostracization.

So, there I was, a nerd without a niche, a challenge, or a friend.

A loner. No way around it.

There wasn't a feeling of belonging for me, anywhere.

Even in the house that was my home, I felt like an outsider.

Continually reminded of the collective lies we told each other every time I put on my Little League Baseball jersey with "Mohammed" and not "Bello" printed squarely on the back.

The whole concept of home for me had begun to blur as I got older and more detached from my responsibilities, both as a brother and a son.

My biological mom, who would still visit occasionally, had become more of an unwelcome sight to me.

She represented an increase in rules and regulations. A tighter eye on all comings and goings. A constant presence over your shoulder who'll occasionally go through your things if she so felt inclined.

In short, I was essentially grounded for the months at a time my mom would visit from London.

My biological dad also visited once. I was five at the time, and don't remember much about the interaction.

So, there's that.

H-E-L-P!

As I already alluded to, friends were tough to come by, and the few I had remained within the walls of school.

I was a geek – not "cool" in the slightest.

Enjoyed reading and competing in school spelling bees, so it wasn't like kids were lining up to hang out.

Well, except for one.

We'll call him DJ.

Our friendship began because of our parents working relationship, and naturally, since we were in the same grade - we became buds.

My mom knowing his mom made it a much easier threshold to cross in terms of doing anything that involved leaving the house.

This may also be a good time to note that I didn't really identify as "black" in the cultural sense.

I didn't play basketball or listen to rap music.

I was in honors classes and wore transition lenses.

I loved learning about space, collecting baseball cards, and turning my homework in on time.

Weird shit.

Anyway, I'll cut to the chase because this is still tough for me to reconcile with, probably why I'm stalling.

I've stuffed it so deeply into my psyche that digging it back up is not very pleasant, but -

DJ was both bigger and stronger than I was.

He would sometimes try and fool around when I was over.

Yes.

Keep in mind, we were both 9. I hadn't even seen porn yet. This was all new to me. So out of fear, I went with it.

I had no real conception for what was going on, but he seemed to.

This went on about a year or so, and for some odd reason my traumatized brain just didn't process that I could say no...

Until, one day he tried to take it too far, and so I hurt him.

We'll just leave it at that.

Basically, I was an actor.

I had no bearings on how to get along with people authentically, and so I found myself in a role that I didn't want to play – but I played it.

Mostly because I wanted someone to hang out with, I think.

There's a lot to unpack there still, but I'll bury those insights until next time. Probably should go talk to a therapist first, but I don't know.

We're all going through it.

Is what it is.

Edumacated

Most of the advanced classes I was in were filled with the overachieving type, 90% white and likely a part of some club that existed outside school.

And, that crowd didn't really vibe with me.

Remember, I had a sheltered life and didn't venture out much. So, with no real luck in finding a group of friends, I found solace in my mental.

I liked to think a lot. Still do.

Read, ponder, write, imagine, dream, whatever to get away from my immediate reality.

Science fiction was (and still is) a personal favorite.

From a young age I'd always been curious about the universe and wanted to better understand our role in this intricate cosmic system we've self-actualized in.

Thinking about space makes me feel *really* small.

And I like that.

So, there's me.

Nerdy kid with the glasses. Crushing on every pretty girl at the school. Writing notes, never sending them.

Looking back, I credit much of my mastery over words to a love for books, and my imagination.

They were the only ones there for me in an odd sense.

Them, and the Churchill Elementary School librarian who continually put me on to new reads. Shoutout to you, whoever you are.

Of course, there were some good teachers sprinkled in too; Ms Boomer, Targen, Searcy and a couple of others. But unfortunately, the vast majority were just not remarkably interesting.

Whether underpaid, overworked, or a combination of these and more; many of my institutional instructors left me thoroughly bored, and so from an early age I decided to do my own thing.

The strategy worked well for a while.

I've always been a good test-taker (which, really isn't important in the grand scheme of things, but still a nice skill to have)

So, school wasn't a problem, and since I wasn't very inclined to be athletically engaged beyond in-house baseball - I had a lot of free time.

Free time that should have been spent exploring and engaging with the world.

But alas, I was cooped up at home. Reading, playing video games, and scheming for the day I could achieve that ever-elusive sense of freedom.

Jesus? Uh...

It was a few years later, about junior high, that I started having serious doubts about my hand me down faith.

What I'd come to adopt was essentially a second-hand Christianity, passed down from my mother – but never really interrogated to become my own.

Growing up in a religious household has some advantages, but in my case, the environment only taught me how to better wear my mask.

My authoritative mother left very little room for dialogue in our relationship. To be sure I never received any sort of 'sex talk', or insight into how relationships work.

What I did get, was a CD of a screaming Nigerian pastor rebuking premarital sex followed by a terrible song about chastity that played on a loop afterward.

My childhood would have been a great study in classical conditioning.

Anyway, my parents and I rarely opened about life outside progress reports, so I tended to keep any more controversial ideas to myself.

This meant pretending to believe God was real vs. *actually* believing God was real. And that did quite a number on my spirit.

Never really had a problem with regurgitating information.

Remember, great test taker.

And not only in school, but with the church folks as well.

I was the kid who memorized every book of the bible by age 10.

Had all the Wednesday service patches on my jacket like I was some sort of boy scout / super Christian hybrid they made in a test tube.

I learned very quickly how to keep up appearances, and though the outside world wasn't aware, my family was starting to catch on to the depravity in my soul, hiding under the thin veneer of good deeds.

Challenge accepted.

This didn't mean we got to talking about feelings.

Lol, no no no.

There is no back and forth between parent and child in Yoruba culture.

Ah ah.

Expectations are set extremely high and often come at the expense of relationship.

So, in order to save face after a few run ins with the parental units, I promptly got my act together and began to truly become the son they always wanted...

...naw, I'm just playing.

Only ramped up the act.

Because, in the absence of authentic connection, I just felt bullied into a corner. Either get in line or get in trouble.

So yeah, I got in line... but only for a bit.

Performances take energy to keep up, and a lot of it.

Plus, you don't feel very appreciated or even recognized afterwards, because the thing is, performance is *expected*.

By this time, I had a pretty marked home/school/church life.

The code switching had become normal, natural even.

And this framing of the Christian life as one dominated by rules and assessed by performance was the version I had grown to believe.

This all culminated to my baptism around age 12.

Another show for the congregation.

Let the church say amen.

Except, it wasn't for me.

It wasn't even for God.

Shortly afterwards, as if to add insult to injury, it came out that the leader of this church (i.e. the guy who dunked my head underwater) had been mismanaging church funds from the coffers to his pockets.

He was then promptly shown the door after the leadership team found out. My already dwindling faith in the institution of 'church' was at this point, justified.

Yet.

I can't help but recognize that the constant barrage of memory verses I learned in Wednesday AWANA services would soon equip me against some of the toughest situations I'd ever have to face.

Or how my apparent house arrests kept me from ever becoming too much of a plotter; because... I had ideas.

So, I suppose I owe the adoptive parental units a big thank you.

You sacrificed a lot to keep me on the straight and narrow, when I didn't want to be there.

And I love you guys for that.

CHAPTER 3:
ME, MYSELF & I

Nobody likes being alone that much. I just don't go out of my way to make friends...

It only leads to disappointment.

Haruki Murakami

I don't want to be alone,

I want to be left alone.

Audrey Hepburn

So, I needed an outlet.

Or at least a person to waste time with.

Finally, around 5th grade I forced myself to make a friend.

He lived a few houses down and didn't try to make me do anything I didn't want to.

Perfect.

We were just normal kids who went to Culver's on half days, ran around local parks on weekends, and played video games late at night.

Honestly, I was surprisingly well behaved all things considered.

Got straight A's, never was in trouble, even made the travel baseball team that year.

And still.

Rejection continued to abound on the school front, as I didn't make the cut for the National Junior Honors Society, even though I was in all advanced classes. (Yes, I know I'm a nerd. I've accepted it.)

But I can't front, that was a blow to the intellectual ego.

It became increasingly difficult to justify caring about this school thing.

(also didn't make the fall play, this after thinking that everyone made them in middle school. So that was some bullshit.)

Fast forward to ninth grade and my social life, or lack thereof, became even more apparently deficient.

I never went downtown.

Parties were few and far between.

I didn't even like to drink, so I couldn't pretend to be cool even if I ever found myself in such a situation.

I was socialized exclusively in parks, basements, movie theatres, and classrooms. Low expectations, minimal drama. Cool with me I guess.

My mental faculties were still there, but fresh off being spurned by an education system that didn't allow me into its 'honors society' I felt that the only way to exist was to take it in stride.

To be a nice guy.

Maybe then people would like me.

I wanted to be popular, only nerds weren't that.

So, I found clubs, joined teams, did activities (so many activities).

Taekwondo, soccer, band [1st chair clarinet 5 years...], football, soccer, track, baseball, swimming & piano lessons on and on and on.

But, with no foundational understanding of the 'why', all were useless.

Like, continuing to pile dirt upon what was already buried.

My 'real' self wanted to break free, but my 'other' self kept me stuck in a cycle of codependence and frustration.

Anyway.

Sanni Iyintosoluwami

Oluwafisayomi Oluwasekemi

Mohammed Haruna

That's my name.

Don't wear it out.

As I got older, it became more a claim to fame than anything else.

Fact is, I wanted to change it. Multiple times.

But, for reasons still beyond my understanding - the process was always delayed and would then magically drop from the realm of parental consciousness after a week or two.

For a while I held a lot of resentment towards my mom for what I deemed a typo on the birth certificate.

Being a "Mohammed" was not my wish in the slightest, especially since I didn't even know the guy.

But like most other things, I eventually lost interest, and feelings of indifference toward everyone and everything were once more reinforced.

Had to learn to stop asking questions, to keep it moving.

And it sucked.

But, gotta say –

In retrospect, glad I never busted out the correction tape. My name represents much more than a familial labeling system.

Like in most cultures, but especially African ones, a name is a sacred thing. It can take upwards of two weeks for a tribe to settle on one, and there are often huge ceremonies that come with the announcement.

Friends and family come together and shout out potential titles as if they're collectors bidding at an auction.

(That's actually not true. I just thought the visual was funny)

Nevertheless, a bunch of people converge.

Then, tada!

African baby with a cool name.

My *real* first name (since "Sanni" is more like a generic placeholder) is Iyintosoluwami.

From where I get my nickname, Toso.

ee-yeen-TOH-SO-loo-wah-me.

Means, 'my God is worthy of praise'.

Beautiful.

But at the time, I hated it.

I resented the fact that my brother was a neatly named 'Anthony' and my sister was an inoffensive 'Gabrielle'

...yet, here I was...

a Toso without a cause.

Before we move on

A defense mechanism I often employ when something doesn't go my way, is simply to block it out.

To not care.

As if the problem or situation has magically vanished.

Not the best tool in the box, but it was the only way I knew how to exist for a while.

My emotional deficiencies are still something I struggle with today, from how I relate to my ex, family and friends, classmates, coworkers, lovers, enemies, and damn near everyone in between.

So, at this point in the story, the relationship between my babysitters (i.e. my 'parents') and I was purely surface level.

I found it amusingly easy to say one thing and to do another. I began to explore sex more, and of course… I was blown away.

The shouting Nigerian pastor didn't say anything about this.

Like, what God are you talking about…?

You mean, the God that lets his kid get molested?

And watched the head pastor steal His money?

Oh. Okay.

I think I'll take it from here then, "God".

CHAPTER 4: TURBULENCE

However mean your life is, meet it and live it; do not shun it and call it hard names.

Henry David Thoreau

If time has beaten you severely and your face is swollen, smile and act like a fat man.

Nigerian Proverb

The summer before junior year, my parents urged me to attend a summer school program at Stanford University.

It was $8,000.

Way too expensive for a lower middle-class family.

Yet my mind immediately went to the fact that I could be "free" for an entire month and a half. So, I accepted the challenge.

Applied that winter and was accepted a few months later.

Keep in mind, my concept of money at the time was elementary at best.

I never got an allowance, or worked a real job, or had a bank account.

Even the times that I would touch money (at church) comprised of the dollar that my mom would hand me as the collection plate got passed.

A formality, nothing more.

And so, I recognized all money as such.

Regardless, I had a blast that summer.

Got to exchange time and energy with people who were extremely intelligent, in a new city, far away from home.

Kissed a girl from Italy, smoked a joint in San Francisco, broke into historic buildings on campus, ran around jumping into fountains.

Oh yeah. And took courses taught by the world's leading minds.

But I was there purely for the experience.

So, based on that – I thought it was a rather successful summer.

Though if you ask my parents, I failed.

Miserably.

(And maybe I did.)

See, I took two courses there. Got an A in one and a C in the other.

Not stellar, but 16-year-old me was let loose in California for six weeks, and the last thing he cared about was being in a classroom or turning in homework. He just wanted to have fun.

Truth be told, I grew a lot.

During the time away, I began to get a taste of what else the world had to offer.

Though, my carefree lifestyle was short lived

Cocoa Butter Kisses

I made friends. I also lost some.

Many connections became strained because of the physical distance, sure. But also, the emotional gap.

I wasn't mature enough to handle the responsibilities of a committed relationship, and my indifference spilled over into dealings of the heart after a few breakups.

I was a kid. In some ways, I still am. Brimming with insecurities.

Had no business in a relationship at that point though, still needed to find out who the hell I was.

Marijuana was a high point to the second half of my journey in self-discovery. Pun intended. But seriously.

It's a beautiful plant.

Helped slow my racing thoughts, granted me peace (albeit artificially), and was the backdrop to some eye-opening conversations with others.

But more importantly, to some conversations with God.

Thus, began my decision to do away with all the extra stuff.

(aka religion)

Quit football senior year since my knees didn't agree anymore.

(Remember those Vibram toe-shoes that were a fad for a while? Yeah, I ran track in those. Every day. Oops)

The apparent silver lining was of course, no practice, i.e. more free time.

Senior year was a lot of me driving the car of my own life. I learned fast not to trust anyone or even consider their attempts to help steer.

I'd grown a healthy skepticism of both the people and institutions that had been long held up in my eyes as infallible, and I began to question a lot of other things too.

Like why in 2012 is formal "education" still a thing?

Or why don't they teach important stuff...

like spiritual development, or how to file taxes?

So, I stopped caring about school to learn and saw it chiefly as a way out of the house.

I became more uninvolved in my role as a brother and a son and saw myself most as an individual.

But the act was getting old.

No one in my nuclear family was impressed by the feigned attempts to 'change', and so they sent me to get 'fixed'.

By the local pastor, Jason Perry.

Mind you, he wasn't the first.

But for some reason, this particular union began what I still feel was a fruitful relationship, the only one in my life at the time that kept me somewhat tethered to God, and away from the chaos which could very well have ensued.

So, I guess I should have some appreciation for that.

Shout out to my folks.

And a big thanks to JP.

Much love, always.

CHAPTER 5:
TEMPTATIONS &
LIMITATIONS

"It does not matter how slowly you go as long as you do not stop"

Confucius

"The worst crime is faking it"

Kurt Cobain

My gifts began to fail me, or maybe I began to fail them.

I could still maintain appearances, even found a sense of redemptive ego coddling in being selected VP of the National Honor Society.

(take that, NJHS)

It couldn't raise my spirits though.

My life was rather empty, if anyone cared to dig around a bit.

I was still a natural, able to beat out a bunch of novices at some international business competition, actually placed 4th in the world, this despite never attending a review session.

I also got a partial scholarship to some law school in Chicago for excelling in Mock Trial, regardless of chronic absenteeism.

If you can't tell by now, the problem wasn't in the activities, but in my lack of purpose behind any of them.

All were simply means to an end.

That end? to *look* competent.

My GPA wasn't great that year, but it held the line.

Senioritis slippage reduced the 4-year average to a 3.3-something. Not nearly enough to impress any of the colleges I applied to.

Since I was more interested in appearing smart than in being so, college acceptance adjudicators at prestigious universities across the U.S., from Brown to Cornell, were not too keen on giving me a shot after seeing my performance dip that second semester.

And ultimately, no Stanford for me either.

What made it worse is that my cousin had just gotten into Harvard the year before... so that was a fun Thanksgiving.

Whole crew goes hard to be fair. The Adeyemi's. Look em up.

Proud doesn't even begin to explain, but things are weird these days.

I keep it uncomfortably real, and don't care much for pats on the back.

Really, I want the freedom to direct myself. Personal sovereignty.

My family wanted recognition. Status.

Our aims were incongruent.

Finally, the University of Minnesota was settled upon.

It was the least expensive of the 'second-tier' schools, and was closest in proximity so I couldn't go too crazy.

But it wasn't a done deal at any point. They were still wary of letting me go a week before classes began.

I didn't even get a graduation party.

I think I'm still bitter, can't lie.

It was an odd time; I had no real clue as to what my future looked like for those three long months.

But -

Despite reservations, Pastor Jason seemed able to convince the folks to give me another chance.

Maybe he lied to them about the growth I was experiencing, or explained how sorry I truly was for blowing their precious $8000.

Regardless, they relented.

Woo?

My roommates were pro-marijuana and anti-authority, so I fit in nicely.

That newfound freedom was too much to resist.

The first night, and for many after.

(Sorry mom.)

Though despite, that year spent in the Twin Cities would become the backdrop to a transformation God was beginning in my life. Don't get me wrong, it was ugly at times.

But I began to learn about things I'd never been able to grapple with before, so it was also necessary.

Having nobody over my shoulder meant I got to call the shots, and with that, bear the consequences.

Time flew, and the end of the school year came way too fast. Naturally, I was struggling to reintegrate back home after months of debauchery.

I ended up going to a concert in Chicago with an old high school friend that weekend, and of course I smoked some weed.

Got home, went to sleep thinking nothing of it.

Next morning, surprise. Drug test.

And poof. Just like that. No more University. I'm a homebody again.

With broken relationships at home, and very little opportunity to reconnect to old friends due to another impending house arrest, I found myself reaching back to Suz for a sense of stability.

Told her some lie about grandma being sick and to pray for her, and it got me in.

Ironic though, how it was a lie that was the foundation of the second iteration in our relationship.

And how this lie, led to a conversation, which eventually led to a marriage... which ended in a divorce.

One little lie. So much avoidable pain.

One of the main reasons it's now hard for me to tolerate dishonesty, is because I learned first-hand just how destructive it can be.

I was caught up rocking the rose-colored goggles for far too long. Thought she saw something in me, and the faith she had dissuaded any temptations of me giving up on becoming a better person.

Problem is it wasn't for me. It was for her.

Oh well.

Because I have made it through that storm and *have* become a better person in the process.

So, I guess... I should be thanking you too, Suzanne.

You stood in the gap and kept my soul clean when I had little reason to do so. And, I love you. Still.

Hope you can forgive me one day.

CHAPTER 6:
RUN IT BACK

"Doing what needs to be done may not make you happy, but it will make you great"

George Bernard Shaw

"Whatever you do, work heartily, as for the Lord and not for men."

Colossians 3:23

Pastor Jason became more heavily involved in my life over the next few years. We'd go back and forth, positing different theological ideals and debating their ramifications in our respective realities.

He was, and still is an instrumental guide in my journey – though, I tended to see him as more of an intellectual guide, than a spiritual one.

Nonetheless, I learned a lot about his views on God, and though we still disagree about a few things, (namely the role of psychedelics in spiritual formation, lol) there's still a healthy level of mutual respect.

After getting pulled out of school that year, I was on my own financially - so going back to Minnesota was out of the question.

I just didn't see any value in education, and thus, wasn't going to take loans which furthered myself along a path I didn't want to be on.

I decided instead to take classes at the local community college, paying my way through with a part time retail job.

Mostly to appease the folks, but also to maintain some routine that didn't involve smoking weed every day.

I figured it had cost me enough at this point and it'd be cool to relax for a bit and prove to everyone that I can be average.

Back to school*

I still didn't take school seriously; it was nearly impossible to.

The classes were easier than the ones I'd taken two years prior in high school, so grades couldn't be the incentive.

A's were entirely too easy to come by.

This time around, instead of finding a bunch of activities to do, I decided to fully invest in one.

My first class at the college was a communications course taught by a high energy instructor by the name of David Naze.

After seeing me give a quick speech for a class assignment, he suggested I join forensics. So, I thought about it, then I did.

(This is forensics as in speech club, not crime scene investigations)

That decision began what has been an awesome journey for me to date, one in which I would grow with confidence and begin to find my own voice amongst recycled takes that proliferate on twitter.

I got to compete at nationals a few times and was able to hear a wide range of unfiltered perspectives in the form of poetry, speeches, and stories that would forever change how I thought about the world.

Also began to rediscover my joy for reading around this time, devouring classics such as CS Lewis' "Mere Christianity".

It was a period of personal development, a time of figuring, and of becoming. I was building out a new foundation.

Though, I endured much of this walk alone.

Suz was still away at Minnesota and I was not. Though honestly, I was oddly okay with this. In retrospect, that was probably a red flag.

Reading, writing, working.

That was my life for ten months.

And it wasn't terrible.

No boat rocking at home, stable relationships beginning to take root, life inching towards stability.

Maybe this is it. Follow the rules and reap the rewards of convenience, not exciting by any means.

But acceptable.

So, I'm grateful I didn't return to Minnesota that year.

I clearly had some growing up to do, and the time home gave me clearer vision for what I wanted to accomplish in this life.

It represented the first time I'd ever done some work on my life for reasons that weren't simply to maintain appearances.

I wasn't trying to further an agenda, or to become more 'likeable'.

I was just finding my footing. Finding myself really.

Books became portals to other perspectives, and I was beginning to operate with the awareness of a bigger plan for my life than what was immediately apparent.

I also realized that I was here to find and accomplish that plan, no matter how difficult. Growth. That's it.

Though, paired with a lot of discomfort. All good.

I have the Creator of the universe in my corner now.

Maybe God ain't so bad.

Back to School

Fall of 2016, I showed up on the campus of ONU, and my former state university experience was about to be quickly replaced by the less appealing trappings of a small, religious, liberal arts college in the middle of nowhere.

Co-ed dorms and frat parties?

Try twice weekly chapel services and an abundance of forced smiles.

It wasn't meant to be fun, not for me at least.

But it was a change I was ready for.

Newly engaged and equally convinced that I needed to complete college and get a degree to be of any value in this world, I went.

Somehow, still managed to find buddies who thumbed their nose at our neat 'bubble' – and despite the strict rules and overbearing public safety patrollers, I still managed to find trouble.

Cigarettes, coffee, weed, and my energetic roommate got me through that first year.

Still missed track meets, and regularly skipped class.

Still smoked as much as I possibly could, given the confines.

And still got dean's list a few semesters.

Old habits were beginning to creep back into focus, but it worked.

Or maybe, God was working in spite of my ignorance.

I even got to intern with the Chicago Bears, who ran summer training on our campus. Met some great people.

But be warned, the work wasn't super fun.

I think I prefer being a fan.

CHAPTER 7: NEW CREATURE

"Therefore, if anyone is in Christ, they are a new creation. The old has gone, the new has come!"

2 Corinthians 5:17

"Every new beginning comes from some other beginning's end."

Seneca

2017 came and went...

no degree.

2018...

Nada.

2019...

Still nothing.

Look at me now.

Impending papers from ONU have been pushed back indefinitely and I have no plans on returning anytime soon.

Since 2018, I've been in flux. Due mainly to an incapability of bringing myself to complete another. pointless. class.

So, I dropped out. With 7 credits to go.

Seriously, it can get that petty with me.

Hundred and some odd hours received from several historic institutions across the United States from California to Illinois.

And not one degree.

What's wild is, they still let me walk the stage at ONU's graduation.

I guess the fake celebration did the trick because I haven't been back since.

It was around this time I felt compelled to look more critically at my own story, so I became part of this small group at a local church called 'The Journey'.

It was comprised of mostly old people, but I liked that. They tend to have more rounded perspectives anyway.

I began to write more, as the group assignments would call for it - and I rediscovered the joy I had for bending words into meaning.

Those quiet moments in the Homewood Public Library (though, I hadn't the slightest clue at the point) were the beginnings of the book that you happen to be reading right now.

Pastor Jason started a new church called C3 and asked me to be a part of building out the groundwork.

His idea was that people today had gotten detached from themselves due to a lack of focus on real relationships, to which I agreed emphatically. Plus, I didn't have a home church at the time, so I joined.

This was the beginning of Connections Cubed, and oddly enough, it was also the beginning of the end of our teacher/student relationship.

(Though I didn't know that yet, either.)

Fast Forward

Okay, you've stuck around long enough.

Let's get this over with.

Proposed to Suzanne the summer of 2016, on some dumb shit.

Or at least, on some short-sighted shit.

Say that 5x fast.

I simply assumed that it was the next logical step – and didn't bother asking myself if I was ready for such a commitment. It had to work.

Still no degree, and so I ended up taking a job at an afterschool facility for teens. Honestly, I loved the kids. But - we'll just leave it at that.

This happened alongside me working with JP to plant that church – and while striving to repair broken relationships left on the home front.

And while moving into a new apartment downtown with the lady I just decided to spend the rest of my life with.

Lots of moving parts.

And only four years later, just about all of them have fallen apart.

The marriage,

The church,

My family life,

And obviously school has been over with.

I've worked a few odd jobs since then to make ends meet.

But truly, I didn't care about any of them.

It was (and still is) hard for me to find the value in this tradeoff between time and money everyone else seems to be cool with.

I just wanted to do the things that I wanted to do.

Money can help me accomplish those things, but not if I'm stuck in an office all day. To me, money is essentially a middleman.

I just wanted to live life more directly.

So, I decided that money will never be an object for me.

I want my wealth to be compounded in unique experiences and genuine relationships, not in paper issued by questionable governments.

Maybe I'm crazy.

Refer to the title page.

I just prefer what's real.

Probably should have let my wife in on that revelation, but of course, love covers all – right?

So, I was back at square one. Only this time, my wife was my mom.

And, it was my own fault. I wanted to use her.

For freedom, for sex, for confidence, for whatever boys get into relationships for these days,

But I didn't do my best to love her.

Not really.

Figured that the attraction I had was enough to hold us together while I got onto bigger plans of saving the world.

What a fool.

Because…

It wasn't. And I didn't.

I worked for nonprofits that still somehow managed to put profits over people. I started a flimsy organization of my own with the wife, before lacking conviction to follow through a couple years in.

I helped facilitate potentially fraudulent research on public school children across the city of Chicago. And I began to realize that if I continued on this trajectory –

I wouldn't simply fall into the good life I'd imagined for myself.

Traveling, learning, experiencing, and loving.

That was the goal.

But at this point, I was moving in the opposite direction.

Planting a garden of weeds while expecting to reap a harvest of flowers.

Except, it doesn't work like that.

(we're almost done, don't worry)

Now, I strive to be a person of integrity.

The same, no matter who you catch me around.

But, still have strained relationships, and feel that time is short.

Yet, continue to struggle to apply myself consistently.

I know that God started a good work in me.

But I'm still early in that walk, and unsure of how 'full maturity' looks.

I know there will be blessings and battles alike.

And now I look forward to them.

I understand that everything viewed through the correct lens, holds potential for creation.

Just as everything when viewed improperly, holds potential for destruction.

The journey is everything, and **your mindset determines your course.**

So, I remain grateful.

Optimistic to what He has in store for my life.

Because at this point, I just want to be a vessel.

I know I'm messed up.

But that's what makes the trip so exciting.

Last thoughts

To those I've failed to communicate with, I apologize.

If I've lashed out in confusion, or have been absent for a bit – I'm sorry.

But please, understand.

I had to get right for myself before doing so for anyone else.

Full disclosure.

I was diagnosed with paranoid schizophrenia in April of 2019.

Honestly, it's still weird for me to think that out loud.

The week I spent in the Advocate Medical psych ward was probably rock bottom for me. At least, one of them.

I was with people who had what felt like real mental health issues.

My roommate lost his son in a drowning accident a year before and couldn't sleep without heavy sedatives.

A woman down the hall would scream at all hours of the night from terrors triggered by thoughts of abusive relationships.

Real demons.

I just smoked weed dude.

Most of the patients in this place looked more like zombies than humans. It was very unsettling.

But somehow, I knew I'd be okay.

It's difficult to explain, especially if you don't believe in God – but the peace I felt during that week was insane.

I'm still not sure how I was able to cope. Physically I was alone, but the whole time there was an energy about me, pushing me along.

It kept me from getting too depressed or explicitly suicidal, I simply maintained. This isn't to say it was easy.

On more than a few occasions, I felt death was close.

Again, it's hard to explain.

But there were periods when I'd suddenly come down with this sense of impending ruin. Almost physical. Like a weighted blanket.

I literally stole a bible from the common area and would sleep with it under my pillow at night just to *feel* at peace.

I didn't get many calls.

A testament to how far I must have gone for those close to me.

Because, the tough truth here is…

people treat you, the way you treat them.

And I had let a lot of people down.

So… only right it happened this way.

For some, I've been absent on purpose.

Had to bust out the scissors for my own wellbeing,

But most? Nah.

I was just negligent.

Is what it is.

Besides, recognizing the problems as having started with me actually became a source of power. The blaming stopped, and the repair began.

I saw that ultimately, I needed to take accountability.

It's the only way I could heal.

So, in closing –

Keep loving, speak truth, and *never stop growing*

Remember that your potential to impact life is greater than you could ever imagine. Don't sell yourself short because others can't see it yet.

Anyway, that's it.

Thanks for stopping by.

EPILOGUE

"There is no real ending. It's just the place where you stop the story."

Frank Herbert

Hey – you made it.

Thanks for taking the time.

If this impacted you in any way, please let me know.

wearehuman.international@gmail.com

I love to hear a good story.

Narratives are an important way we learn.

About ourselves, about the world, about others.

So today, I strongly urge you to begin working on your own.

Seriously.

Because, I want to live in a world filled with people who *act from the truth* of who they are, and not based in some label they were assigned.

Too often, the identities you've grown to adopt become bumpers to your being. Guardrails that can restrict you over time and make you less and less yourself.

Right now, you have a choice to make about who you'll allow to dictate the rest of your existence on Earth.

You can literally be anyone you want these days.

But, why not try and be yourself?

You've gotta dig, and I'm not saying it'll be easy.

Just, necessary.

Knowing where you are from, will give you better clues of where to go. Your future is simply a continuation of a story which you author.

Remember –

Map it.

Calibrate it.

Then move forward.

If you don't know how to start, begin by listing events that were important to your development.

Big or small. Doesn't matter. Just, have to be real.

Then, organize them in a way that makes sense.

(Chronologically works but I have seen it thematically as well.)

After you have a healthy list of 30-50 events that have been somewhat organized, you've effectively created a rough draft of your own story.

Boom.

Now, give those events meaning.

Really the medium is up to you.

BUT –

Personally, I like writing.

So - if you need help in that department or would like to bounce ideas off someone interested in seeing you grow – hit me up on Patreon.

https://www.patreon.com/humankind

My life's mission is to impact souls by getting people to recognize the truth of who they are.

The beautiful you that's been hiding,

Is exactly who the world is waiting for.

So, stop holding out.

It's time to be.

And please know,

I love you.

Appreciate you sticking around.

Now go and be you.

Printed in Great Britain
by Amazon

37723733R00030